THE *Virginia* COLONY

Our Thirteen Colonies

SPIRIT
of America®

THE *Virginia* COLONY

By Sarah E. De Capua

Content Adviser: Eric Gilg, Department of History, University of
Massachusetts, Amherst, Massachusetts

The Child's World®
Chanhassen, Minnesota

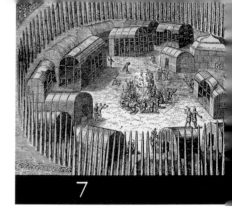

7

THE *Virginia* COLONY

Published in the United States of America by The Child's World®
PO Box 326 • Chanhassen, MN 55317-0326 • 800-599-READ • www.childsworld.com

Acknowledgments
The Child's World®: Mary Berendes, Publishing Director

Editorial Directions, Inc.: E. Russell Primm, Editorial Director; Melissa McDaniel, Line Editor; Elizabeth K. Martin, Assistant Editor; Olivia Nellums, Editorial Assistant; Susan Hindman, Copy Editor; Joanne Mattern, Proofreader; Kevin Cunningham, Peter Garnham, Ruthanne Swiatkowski, Fact Checkers; Tim Griffin/IndexServ, Indexer; Cian Loughlin O'Day, Photo Researcher; Linda S. Koutris, Photo Selector

Photo
Cover: North Wind Picture Archives; Art Resource: 33; Art Resource/National Portrait Gallery, Smithsonian Institution: 28, 29; Bettmann/ Corbis: 10, 18, 24, 35; Bridgeman Art Library: 19 (Roy Mile Fine Painting), 21 (New York Historical Society); Corbis: 9 (The Mariner's Museum), 15 (David G. Houser), 20 (Historical Picture Archive); Getty Images/Hulton Archive: 6, 12, 13, 14, 16, 17, 26, 27; North Wind Picture Archives: 22, 23, 30, 34; Stock Montage: 7, 11, 25.

Library of Congress Cataloging-in-Publication Data
De Capua, Sarah.
  The Virginia Colony / by Sarah E. De Capua.
    p. cm. — (Our colonies)
  "Spirit of America."
  Includes bibliographical references (p.) and index.
  Contents: Before Europeans—Exploration and settlement—Becoming a colony—During the war—After the war and nationhood—Time line—Glossary terms.
  ISBN 1-56766-711-2 (alk. paper)
  1. Virginia—History—Colonial period, ca. 1600–1775—Juvenile literature. 2. Virginia—History—1775–1865—Juvenile literature. [1. Virginia—History—Colonial period, ca. 1600–1775. 2. Virginia—History—1775–1865.] I. Title. II. Series.
  F229.D33 2003
  975.5'02—dc21   2003003777

12   20   30

Contents

Chapter ONE

Before Europeans

In this painting, the artist imagines what life was like for Native Americans who hunted in the abundant forests, as the Algonquians did in what is now Virginia.

HAVE YOU EVER WONDERED WHAT THE UNITED States was like before it became the United States? How do you think the land looked before there were roads and highways, cities and towns, houses and office buildings? For thousands of years before the arrival of Europeans, Native Americans lived in North America. Their ways of life differed, depending on where they lived. For example, Native Americans of the Northwest got much of their food from the sea. For the Native Americans of the Plains, far from the sea, the largest source of food was the buffalo.

In the area that is now Virginia, most Native Americans belonged to the Algonquian nation, the largest native group in North America. Most of the Algonquian lived in small tribes scattered across the area. They lived by hunting, fishing in rivers, making maple sugar in the spring, and growing crops such as peas, beans, squash, and corn. They were not **nomads,** but they did move their villages a few times each year. The tribes were led by councils of chiefs and elders. War was common among the tribes, occurring nearly every year, usually in the summer.

The homes of Native American villages were often protected by high posts known as palisades. An engraving by Theodor de Bry from 1590 shows one such village in Virginia.

One group of 32 tribes inhabited the coastal region of present-day Virginia. This group called itself the Powhatan, after their leader. They had a population of about 13,000. The Powhatan lived in about 200 permanent villages along today's Chesapeake Bay. Their homes were called longhouses, tunnel-shaped buildings made of bark, trees, and branches. Several families lived in each longhouse.

At the head of each tribe was a chief. The chiefs were led by the great chief, Powhatan, who had organized the tribes into a **confederation.**

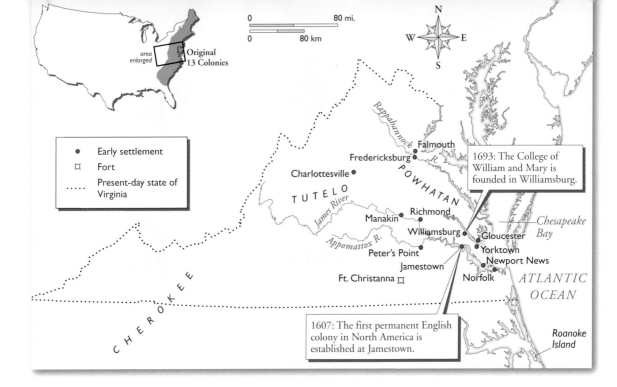

Virginia Colony at the time of the first European settlement

The huge size of the confederation made it possible for the Powhatan to call on large numbers of warriors at any time and to make powerful attacks on enemies. This was especially useful when the Europeans arrived. From 1607, when the first English settlers landed on the coast, to 1646, the Powhatan staged occasional attacks in an attempt to drive them from the region. At times, hundreds of settlers were killed. However, the English responded by sending larger numbers of men and more powerful weapons to fight the Native Americans.

Through the years, peace treaties were made and broken by both the settlers and the Native Americans. By 1669, the Powhatan population dropped to about 1,800. Part of this was due to the many new diseases that colonists brought to the New World. Native Americans had not been exposed to these diseases before, and millions died throughout North America. By 1722, many of the original native groups of Virginia no longer existed. Some tribes lost their lands, while others blended in with the colonial society.

Today, Powhatan descendants live on reservations near the Virginia coast. They share the unique crafts, dances, and traditions of their ancestors with 21st-century visitors.

Interesting Fact

▶ Pocahontas, whose real name was Matoaka, was the daughter of Powhatan.

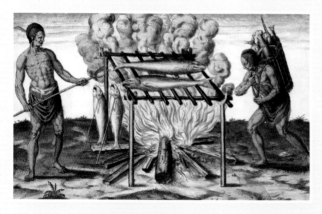

Life of the Powhatan

POWHATAN MEN FISHED, TRAPPED, and hunted animals for food and clothing and made weapons and farming tools. Women made pottery and wooden plates, tended gardens, and gathered food such as nuts and berries. They grew grapes, corn, pumpkins, squash, sunflowers, and beans. They made clothing for everyone in the tribe.

Powhatan children were raised by their mothers. When boys were old enough, their fathers taught them to hunt, fish, and make tools and weapons. When girls reached the right age, their mothers taught them to garden, cook, and make clothing.

Chapter TWO

Exploration and Settlement

CROATOAN. CARVED ON A GATEPOST, THIS WORD, the name of a local native group, was the only sign left behind by the English colonists who settled on Roanoke Island in 1587. Located off the coast of present-day South Carolina, the island colony was begun by Sir Walter Raleigh.

An artist's drawing of colonists arriving at Roanoke Island, from the 1500s.

For the next three years, Raleigh tried to send supplies and more settlers to the colony. But England was at war with Spain, and it wasn't safe for English ships to sail across the Atlantic. When a new expedition finally arrived at Roanoke in 1590, the colonists had disappeared. Although they may have been killed by Native Americans, no one knows exactly what happened to them. Today, the colony is known as the Lost Colony.

The failure of Raleigh's colony kept the English from attempting further settlement of the New World. By 1603, however, England and Spain were at peace. James I was the king of England. Trade was increasing between Europe and Asia. Merchants were getting wealthy from the busy trade. A group of merchants in England banded together in 1606. They formed the Virginia Company of London. At this time, Virginia referred to all the land claimed by the English along the Atlantic coast of North America, between today's Canada and Florida. The men who formed the Virginia Company hoped to make more money from

Sir Walter Raleigh, navigator, historian, and poet, was born in 1554. He traveled to many far lands for England, but he was beheaded in 1618 after angering the king of Spain.

the riches—especially gold—that they believed would be found in Virginia. (It was later determined that there was no gold in Virginia.)

The Virginia Company paid for three wooden ships and 144 men and boys to journey to the New World. The ships, called *Susan Constant, Godspeed,* and *Discovery,* set sail from England on December 20, 1606. The company hoped to establish the first permanent English colony in North America.

After setting sail, the ships followed a south-westerly route across the Atlantic Ocean toward the West Indies. From there, they headed north up the Atlantic coast. On April 26, 1607, after a four-month voyage, they arrived at Chesapeake Bay, between present-day Virginia and Maryland. Only 100 colonists survived the difficult journey.

The colonists sailed across the bay to the mouth of a wide river. They named it the James River, in honor of the king. For two weeks,

The second attempt to settle a Virginia colony brought three ships to the Chesapeake Bay, as depicted in this old engraving.

they sailed up the river, exploring the area and looking for a good place to settle. The Native Americans they encountered called their ships "floating islands."

On May 13, 1607, the three ships anchored off a **peninsula** in the James River. The next day, they went ashore for the first time. The men went to work cutting down trees to build a fort. They also built a triangle-shaped wall around the fort for protection and a storage building for their supplies. They planted corn on the land they cleared. They named their settlement Jamestown. A governing council was set up. The council members had been chosen ahead of time back in

Fearing attack by Native Americans, the Jamestown colonists worked hard to build their fort and create a safe place to settle.

Conditions at Jamestown were so terrible that it came to be known as "the starving time."

London by the Virginia Company. They were named in a secret letter that was opened after the colonists arrived in Virginia.

Jamestown turned out to be a bad location for a settlement. The area was low-lying marshland where mosquitoes bred. As a result, most of the colonists suffered from malaria. There was no source of fresh water. (The James River was salty when the tide was high and muddy when the tide was low.) The colonists' crops took time to ripen. The colonists couldn't leave the fort to hunt or fish because of attacks by Native Americans. Hunger, scurvy, and digestive problems plagued Jamestown. Throughout the summer, as many as three or four colonists died each day. By September, nearly half the colonists were dead, and the colony was almost out of supplies.

COLONIST JAMES PERCY WROTE, "THE FIFTEENTH OF JUNE, WE HAD BUILT and finished our Fort." It measured 420 feet (128 meters) long on the side that faced the river. It was 300 feet (91 m) long on each of the other two sides. A main gate faced the river. At each corner of the long side, watch towers were built with cannons at the top.

Along each inside wall of the fort stood a row of houses. The colonists also built a storehouse, a guardhouse, and a church.

In 1996, archaeologists discovered the remains of the fort, as well as many artifacts, including the skeleton of one of the colonists. In 2002, English armor was found at the bottom of an excavated well. Research continues in the area.

Jamestown has been part of the Colonial National Historical Park since 1936. It is owned and operated by both the United States National Park Service and the Association for the Preservation of Virginia Antiquities. A re-creation of the fort is open to the public throughout the year. More than a million people visit each year to learn what life was like for the colonists.

Chapter THREE

Becoming a Colony

Tobacco became an important crop for Virginia early on in the history of the colony

IN SPITE OF THE DANGERS AND DIFFICULTIES, Jamestown survived. Each year, the Virginia Company sent more colonists and supplies to the tiny settlement. In 1610, the Virginia Company replaced the governing council with a single governor, Sir Thomas West, Lord De La Warr. In 1612, colonist John Rolfe perfected the kind of

tobacco the Native Americans had been growing. Within a few years, tobacco was the main crop in the colony. It was grown on large farms called plantations. Tobacco exporting brought so much money to the colony that by 1619, Jamestown could support itself. New settlements began to grow outside the original site.

In 1619, the first large group of women arrived in Jamestown. Couples married and families were established. That same year, the first black servants arrived aboard a Dutch ship. At first, they were **indentured servants** who took their place in society when their years of service were completed. Years later, indentured servitude became slavery. Slaves

The very first women who came to Jamestown from England, a married woman and her young maid, arrived in 1608 on a supply ship. Many more women came to the colony in later years.

The House of Burgesses was the first legislative assembly in the American colonies.

Interesting Fact

▸ A charter is a formal document that states the rights or duties of a group of people.

were not usually given their freedom.

Also in 1619, the Virginia Company ended sole rule by a governor and gave the colonists a voice in their own government. The company sent a new governor, Sir George Yeardley, to Jamestown. There, according to the company's charter, he formed an assembly. The assembly decided what items would be taxed and how much money colonists would pay in taxes. The assembly was made up of the governor's council (appointed by the Virginia Company) and a House of Burgesses, whose members would be elected by the colonists. Two men would represent each plantation or settlement in the House of Burgesses. These men would be elected by adult men who were landowners. Women, blacks, indentured servants, and men who did not own land could not vote. Even the sons of wealthy plantation owners could not vote until they owned their own farms. Men voted at the county's courthouse by stating their vote out loud, in front of the candidates.

Plantation owners spent a lot of time in public service, as well as on their lands. They worked in their churches, in county courts, or as members of the House of Burgesses. These positions paid little, if any, money. But the planters were glad to have this work. This way, they were able to ensure that the laws and courts protected the rights of property owners.

The first assembly met on July 30, 1619. The assembly exists today as Virginia's state legislature. It is the oldest lawmaking assembly in the Americas and one of the oldest in the world. This assembly recognized that Englishmen in the Americas had a right to take part in their own government, just as Englishmen in England did. The other 12 English colonies that soon formed along the Atlantic coast followed Virginia's example.

Because he was upset with the way the Virginia Colony was being run, King James I took away the colonists' charter and the settlement became a royal colony.

Although the Virginia colony seemed to be making progress, King James became unhappy with the way the Virginia Company was running it. In May 1624, the king canceled the company's charter and made Virginia a royal colony. The king was now in charge of appointing the governor and council. At first, he discontinued the

Unfortunately, as the Virginia tobacco industry grew rapidly in the late 1600s, more and more enslaved workers were required to keep the plantations running. But many early Americans were deeply against this terrible practice.

Interesting Fact

▶ The plantation homes of George Washington, called Mount Vernon, and Thomas Jefferson, called Monticello, have been restored and preserved. Visitors from all over the world tour these homes every year.

House of Burgesses, but it was renewed in 1629.

Meanwhile, Virginia settlers continued to spread westward along the James and York Rivers, and north and south along the Rappahannock and Appomattox Rivers. In 1625, Virginia's population was 1,209 white men, 268 white women, and 23 blacks. Just 10 years later, there were almost 5,000 white settlers in Virginia. They prospered, growing vegetables, including corn and squash, on their farms, and eating plenty of hogs, poultry, and **game.** They continued to grow tobacco, create roads, and clear the forest for more farmland.

By the late 1600s and early 1700s, there were a few wealthy families in Virginia. They lived in comfort, with slaves to work their plantations. These families gained wealth as tobacco growers and merchants. Their homes were large and were decorated with furniture, china, and silver from England. Servants or slaves worked in the large kitchens, which were usually separate from the main houses because of the danger of fire.

20

Wealthy families traveled in large carriages pulled by two or four horses. When the planters weren't running the business of their estates or serving their communities, they hunted, raced horses, and played card games. The Virginia assembly met at Williamsburg, where the capital was moved from Jamestown in 1698. In Williamsburg, balls, plays, and concerts were common. Some planters, such as Thomas Jefferson, were musicians. They enjoyed entertaining guests at their homes.

Although tobacco plantations were at the heart of Virginia's farming culture during the 1700s, most farmers owned only small pieces of land, which they worked themselves.

Most Virginia colonists, however, lived on small farms and worked the land themselves. Husbands, children, and sometimes wives worked in the fields growing corn, wheat, and vegetables. The farmer's wife often spun linen thread from flax grown on the farm and woolen thread from the family's sheep. She would then weave cloth to make clothing for her family.

Carpenters, tailors, blacksmiths, shoemakers, and other skilled tradesmen worked throughout

The College of William and Mary, founded in 1693, is the second-oldest institution of higher learning in North America.

the colony. Their services were always needed. Some worked on plantations, while others set up their shops in farming communities.

Most farmers taught their own children reading, writing, and arithmetic. The children of wealthy planters, however, were educated at home by tutors. They were often the only children to continue their schooling beyond the elementary grades. These wealthy children would attend schools that were usually run by a church. The sons of the wealthiest planters were sent to England to study law or medicine. In 1693, the College of William and Mary was founded in Middle Plantation (later renamed Williamsburg). Today, it is the second-oldest college in the United States.

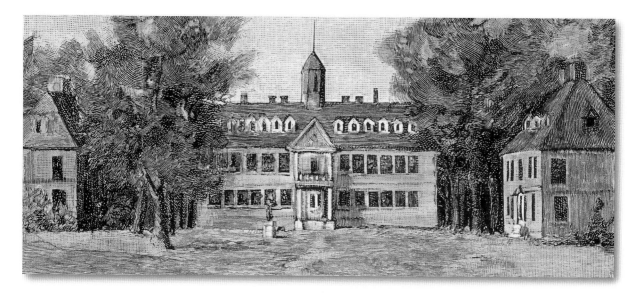

VIRGINIA'S CHARTER GAVE THE COLONY THE lands west and northwest of the areas along the Virginia coast. Virginia's land extended all the way to the Pacific Ocean, but no one knew exactly how much land that included. Virginia claimed land that is now West Virginia, Pennsylvania, Ohio, Indiana, Illinois, Kentucky, and Michigan. Until the 1750s, these claims were meaningless. But they grew more important as settlers from the 13 colonies of Britain spread into lands that were also claimed by France.

In 1753, the French built forts near present-day Pittsburgh, Pennsylvania. The British government ordered Virginia's governor to tell the French to leave the area. Governor Robert Dinwiddie sent 21-year-old **militiaman** George Washington to confront the French. When the French refused to leave, Washington was put in charge of a troop of men and ordered to force out the French. Washington and his men were attacked by the French at a place called Great Meadows and were defeated. Washington and his soldiers returned to Virginia.

Great Britain then decided to send a large force of British soldiers, called Redcoats, to capture the fort. Led by General Edward Braddock, the troops were defeated by the French, who were aided by the Native Americans. Washington, who fought with Braddock, twice narrowly missed being killed.

After Braddock's defeat, Governor Dinwiddie placed Washington in charge of Virginia's soldiers. Constant fighting took place between the colonists and the Native Americans, who were determined to rid the **frontier** of the colonists. Washington and his troops finally defeated the French in 1763, in what became known as the French and Indian War. It was during these battles that Washington gained the experience he needed to lead the American Revolution (1775–1783).

Chapter FOUR

During the War

King George III looked to the colonies to help pay for the debt incurred by fighting the French and Indian War.

WITH BRITAIN'S VICTORY OVER THE FRENCH IN 1763, huge new territories had to be governed. England had gone deeply into debt to win the war. Money was needed to pay the debts, as well as to pay for the army and navy that were required to protect and defend the large area. England's King George III believed the colonists should help to pay these costs.

To raise money, Parliament (Britain's lawmaking body) passed the Stamp Act in March 1765. It required a stamp on every newspaper and official document. Licenses couldn't be issued, ships couldn't sail with goods, and courts couldn't conduct business without a stamp. The Stamp Act would affect nearly every colonist every day.

Virginia's colonists were outraged. Patrick Henry, a member of the House of Burgesses, led the opposition to the act. Colonists in Virginia and the other 12 colonies refused to pay the tax, and Parliament repealed, or officially ended, it.

Parliament didn't give up on taxing the colonists, however. It imposed taxes on glass, paper, tea, sugar, and other products. Colonial trade was heavily taxed. Again, Virginia led the colonial opposition until all the taxes were repealed, except the one on tea. In 1773, colonists in Boston, Massachusetts, responded to the tea tax by dumping a ship's cargo of tea into Boston Harbor. Following this protest, known as the Boston Tea Party, Parliament took a series of harsh actions against Massachusetts, which

While many colonists hoped to find an easy peace with Britain, Patrick Henry spoke out strongly against giving in to English demands. He believed it was timid and unrealistic to think things would improve.

Interesting Fact

▸ The colonists who staged the Boston Tea Party disguised themselves as Native Americans and sneaked onto three ships during the night of December 16, 1773. In all, they dumped 342 chests of tea into Boston Harbor.

included sending Redcoats to occupy Boston. Parliament further angered the colonists when land was taken away from the 13 colonies and made part of the Canadian province of Quebec.

By 1774, the colonies decided to band together to protest Britain's treatment of them. Representatives from each colony formed a Continental Congress in Philadelphia, Pennsylvania. Virginia's representatives included Richard Henry Lee, Patrick Henry, and George Washington. The **delegates** to the Congress agreed that the colonies would stop buying British goods.

The Virginia assembly met in March 1775. It was there that Patrick Henry gave a speech that included the famous words, "Give me liberty, or give me death." Shortly after, in April 1775, the first battles of the Revolutionary War were fought at Lexington and Concord, Massachusetts.

The Second Continental Congress met in Philadelphia less than a month after the war started. Virginia's delegation was one of the largest. On May 15,

The members of the First Continental Congress came together to design a plan of resistance against the British government, which they felt was harsh and unreasonable in its treatment of the colonies.

1776, Virginia was the second colony, after North Carolina, to instruct its delegates to vote for independence from Britain. Since Virginia was the largest and most respected colony, its vote was the most important in the cause for independence.

On June 7, Virginia delegate Richard Henry Lee introduced a **motion** in the Congress that the colonies should declare their independence. On July 2, the motion was adopted. Two days later, on July 4, 1776, the Congress adopted the Declaration of Independence. The Declaration was written by Virginia planter, lawyer, and delegate Thomas Jefferson. It was signed by all the members of the Continental Congress. Besides Jefferson, Virginia's delegates were Richard Henry Lee, George Wythe, Benjamin Harrison, Thomas Nelson Jr., Francis Lightfoot Lee, and Carter Braxton.

The war progressed. It was fought mostly in New York, New Jersey, and Pennsylvania. The British avoided, as much as possible, battling the colonists in Virginia and Massachusetts. The

Richard Henry Lee made the motion for the colonies to declare their independence from Britain.

Interesting Fact

▸ Thomas Jefferson wrote the Declaration of Independence between June 11 and June 28.

British knew these colonies were centers of the Revolution, where anti-British feelings were strong. Colonists there were most determined and ready to fight for freedom. The war did reach Virginia soil, however.

For a short time in 1781, the British controlled much of the Virginia colony. They raided Charlottesville, in an effort to capture the members of the Virginia legislature. The members escaped, but Thomas Jefferson, who was by then the governor of Virginia, was nearly captured in his home at Monticello.

That same year, British general Charles Cornwallis and his force took control of Yorktown, a village on the York River near the Chesapeake Bay. Some of his troops were stationed at Gloucester, on the other side of the York River. Cornwallis waited for more troops and supplies to arrive by sea, but the French, who began fighting on the Americans' side in 1777, sent a fleet to the entrance of Chesapeake Bay. British ships carrying supplies

Thomas Jefferson deeply desired freedom for the colonies, but he was very much against creating a large central government and remained so for his entire life.

and soldiers were stopped from reaching Cornwallis. Washington and his troops then attacked Cornwallis by land. On October 19, 1781, Cornwallis surrendered. In 1782, Great Britain recognized America's independence. The following year, the war was officially ended by the Treaty of Paris.

PATRICK HENRY HAD BEEN SERVING IN THE VIRGINIA House of Burgesses for only nine days in 1765 when he proposed that the House adopt a statement denouncing, or publicly criticizing, the Stamp Act. Henry had already gained a reputation as an effective speaker against the king and his mismanagement of the colonies. However, his suggestion that his fellow burgesses support an official statement against the king was shocking. Some accused Henry of **treason.** But he didn't care what other people thought or said. He believed in the rights of Virginians to conduct their own affairs through their elected representatives and not be ordered about by Parliament.

Patrick Henry's powerful arguments convinced his fellow burgesses to pass strongly worded resolutions declaring the rights of the colonists as Englishmen to tax themselves. Called the Virginia Resolves, they were circulated throughout the colonies and praised by all who heard them. The Resolves were such a powerful statement of the people's rights that they influenced the Declaration of Independence that was to follow.

Chapter FIVE

After the War and Nationhood

After the House of Burgesses no longer existed, this building it had used in Williamsburg, Virginia, became the state capitol.

VIRGINIA ADOPTED A STATE CONSTITUTION IN 1776. It provided for a governor who would be elected by the assembly for one year at a time. The governor had almost no power. All of the power was in the House of Burgesses.

Thomas Jefferson and other leaders wanted Virginia to be a freer, more democratic state. In December 1776, the legislature adopted a Bill of Rights. This guaranteed freedom of the press and of assembly and guaranteed the right to trial by jury. Ten years later, Jefferson's Statute for Religious Liberty was adopted. It guaranteed freedom of religion in Virginia.

Just as Virginia needed a constitution, the new United States of America needed one, too. In 1781, the Articles of

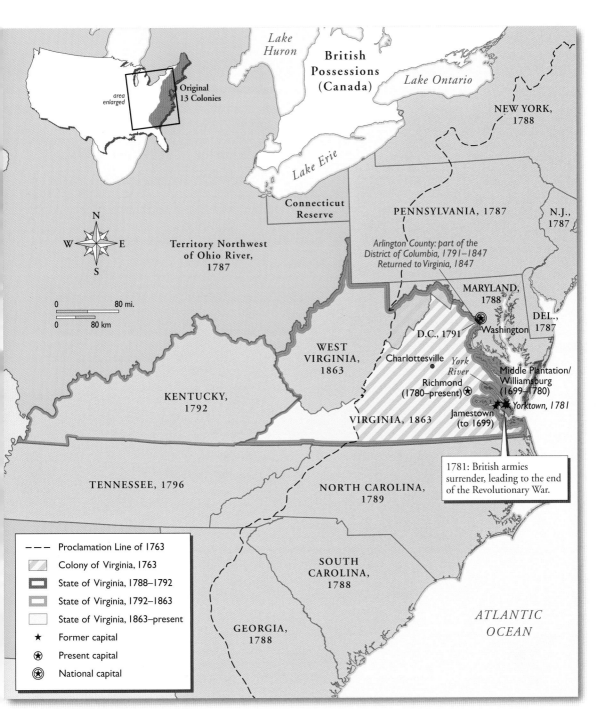

Virginia Colony before statehood

Confederation were approved. However, this provided for a weak central government. It had no chief executive, or leader, no power to tax or trade, and no courts. The leaders of the Revolution believed that the new country could survive only with a strong central government.

In 1787, representatives from every state except Rhode Island met in Philadelphia. They formed the Constitutional Convention. Virginia was a leader in bringing the states together. George Washington, head of the Virginia delegates, was chosen to lead the convention. Another Virginian, James Madison, would also prove to be an important member of the convention.

Virginia developed and presented the Virginia Plan, which Madison wrote. It provided for a national legislature of two houses. The lower house would be elected by the people. The upper house would be elected by members of the lower house. Both houses would elect a chief executive. The legislature, to be called Congress, could make rules on taxes and trade. It also could veto, or reject, laws passed by state governments.

Many delegates to the Constitutional Convention opposed the Virginia Plan. They believed it gave too much power to the central government. The smaller states feared they would have no voice in a Congress in which votes depended on population. New Jersey led the smaller states to propose a different plan. Their plan gave equal voice to all the states and less power to the central government.

George Washington and James Madison led the representatives to a compromise in September 1787. A constitution was drafted that provided for the government we know today. The president would be chosen by electors. The two-house Congress would be made up of a House of Representatives and a Senate. In the Senate, every state would have two votes. In the House, votes would depend on a state's population. The federal government would have its own courts.

The Constitutional Convention decided that each state should hold a convention to ratify, or accept, the Constitution. As soon as nine states ratified it, it would become law.

The members of the Constitutional Convention of 1787 did not originally plan to develop a new form of government. But they soon realized that major changes would be needed to solve the young nation's many challenges.

Because he was willing to compromise, James Madison helped bring the U.S. Constitution into being. Delegates from other states followed his lead.

Delaware was the first state to ratify the Constitution. Americans waited anxiously, however, to find out whether Virginia would ratify. Washington and Madison favored ratification. Patrick Henry and George Mason, a leader in the Revolution, opposed it. Thomas Jefferson was in France as the American **ambassador** at the time, and he was not sure he supported ratification.

Virginia's state convention was held in June 1788. By then, eight states had ratified the Constitution. Virginia's representatives argued for and against the Constitution for nearly a month. One of the biggest arguments against the Constitution was its lack of a Bill of Rights, similar to the one found in Virginia's constitution and the constitutions of other states. Finally, Madison and other supporters agreed to a compromise. The Constitution would be ratified as long as they were allowed to work for an amendment, or change, to the Constitution that provided for a Bill of Rights. Virginia ratified the Constitution. The representatives didn't know that New Hampshire had by then become the ninth state to ratify it, so the Constitution had already become the law of the land. As a result, Virginia, the first colony in the New World, became the 10th state of the United States. The remaining three states ratified the Constitution by 1790.

The states of Virginia and Maryland both donated land along the Potomac River that would become the nation's capital. Virginia made another important contribution to the new nation. When the first presidential election was held in 1788, George Washington was unanimously elected. He was sworn in at Federal Hall in New York City on April 30, 1789. Since then, seven other Virginians have become president of the United States, including Thomas Jefferson—more than from any other state.

From the earliest days of settlement to the making of a nation, the people of Virginia have helped to steer the course of American history and made lasting contributions to the United States.

George Washington was the strong favorite for president because he had contributed so much to the formation of the vibrant new nation.

1587   English settlers establish a colony on Roanoke Island, off present-day North Carolina.

1590   An expedition arrives at Roanoke, only to find the settlers had disappeared.

1606   Merchants form the Virginia Company of London; in December, three ships leave London bound for Virginia.

1607   The first permanent English colony in North America is established at Jamestown.

1610   The Virginia Company replaces Jamestown's ruling council with a governor.

1612   John Rolfe begins to grow an improved tobacco that makes the colony self-sufficient.

1619   The first large group of women, as well as black indentured servants, arrives at Jamestown; Sir George Yeardley arrives as governor, and an assembly is set up.

1624   King James makes Virginia a royal colony.

1693   The College of William and Mary is founded in Williamsburg.

1753–1763   Conflict between the British and French leads to the French and Indian War.

1765   The British Parliament passes the Stamp Act; the Virginia House of Burgesses passes the Virginia Resolves.

1773   Anti-British sentiment spreads through the colonies; colonists in Boston stage the Boston Tea Party.

1774   The first meeting of the Continental Congress occurs in Philadelphia, Pennsylvania.

1775   The Revolutionary War begins with battles at Lexington and Concord, Massachusetts; the Second Continental Congress meets in Philadelphia.

1776   Virginia's delegates to the Continental Congress are instructed to vote for independence. Virginia delegate Richard Henry Lee introduces a motion for independence. Lee's motion is adopted. The Declaration of Independence, written by delegate Thomas Jefferson, is adopted.

1781   British troops control Virginia for a short time during the Revolution; Cornwallis surrenders to Washington; the United States adopts the Articles of Confederation.

1782   Great Britain recognizes America's independence.

1783   The Treaty of Paris officially ends the American Revolution.

1787   The Constitutional Convention meets in Philadelphia.

1788   Virginia ratifies the Constitution; George Washington is elected the first president of the United States.

1936   Jamestown and Yorktown Battlefield become part of the Colonial National Historical Park.

1996   Archaeologists discover the remains of Jamestown fort and artifacts from the settlement.

2002   Armor and other artifacts are found in an excavated well at Jamestown.

Glossary TERMS

ambassador (am-BASS-uh-dur)
An ambassador is the top person sent by a government to represent it in another country. Thomas Jefferson served as U.S. ambassador to France.

confederation (kuhn-fed-er-AY-shun)
A confederation is a union of tribes with a common goal. Powhatan organized different tribes into a confederation.

delegates (DEL-uh-guhts)
Delegates are people who represent other people at a meeting. Patrick Henry and George Washington were two Virginian delegates to the Continental Congress.

frontier (fruhn-TEER)
The frontier is the far edge of a country, where few people live. Native Americans fought against settlers on the frontier of the colonies.

game (GAME)
Game is wild animals, including birds, that are hunted for sport and food. Farmers in colonial Virginia hunted game to eat.

indentured servants (in-DEN-churd SER-vuhnts)
Indentured servants are people who sign and are bound by a formal contract to work for other people for a certain period of time, in return for payment of travel expenses. Some of the first blacks arrived in Virginia as indentured servants.

militiaman (muh-LISH-uh-man)
A militiaman is a member of a militia, citizens trained to fight, but who only serve in times of emergency. George Washington served as a militiaman in the French and Indian War.

motion (MOH-shun)
A motion is a formal suggestion made at a meeting. The Second Continental Congress adopted a motion to declare independence from Britain.

nomads (NOH-mads)
Nomads are people who wander from place to place. The Algonquian people were not nomads, but they did move their villages several times a year.

peninsula (puh-NIN-suh-luh)
A peninsula is a piece of land that sticks out from a larger landmass and is completely surrounded by water. The Jamestown settlement was built on a peninsula in the James River.

treason (TREE-suhn)
Treason is the crime of betraying one's country by helping an enemy. Some people accused Patrick Henry of treason when he opposed the Stamp Act.

37

Virginia Colony's FOUNDING FATHERS

John Blair Jr. (1732–1800)
State court judge, 1777–78; Virginia court of appeals justice, 1779–89; Constitutional Convention delegate, 1787; U.S. Constitution signer

Benjamin Harrison (1726?–1791)
(also known as "The Signer") Continental Congress delegate, 1774–78; Declaration of Independence signer, 1776; Virginia house of representatives member, 1776–82, 1787–91; Virginia speaker of the house of representatives, 1778–82, 1785, 1786; Virginia governor, 1782–84

Patrick Henry (1736–1799)
Continental Congress delegate, 1774–76; Virginia governor, 1776–79, 1784–86

Thomas Jefferson (1743–1826)
Continental Congress delegate, 1775–76, 1783–85; wrote and presented first draft of Declaration; Declaration of Independence signer; Virginia governor, 1779–81; U.S. secretary of state, 1790–93; U.S. vice president, 1797–1801; U.S. president, 1801–09

Francis Lightfoot Lee (1734–1797)
Continental Congress delegate, 1775–79; Declaration of Independence signer; Articles of Confederation signer; Virginia state legislature member, 1780

Richard Henry Lee (1732–1794)
Continental Congress delegate, 1774–79, 1784–89; president of congress, 1784–85; Declaration of Independence signer; Virginia state legislature member, 1779–84; Articles of Confederation signer

James Madison Jr. (1751–1836)
Continental Congress delegate, 1780–83, 1787–88; Constitutional Convention delegate, 1787; U.S. Constitution signer; U.S. House of Representatives member, 1789–97; U.S. secretary of state, 1801–09; U,S, president, 1809–17

Thomas Nelson Jr. (1738–1789)
Continental Congress delegate, 1775–77, 1779; Declaration of Independence signer; Virginia governor, 1781

Edmund Jennings Randolph (1753–1813)
Virginia state attorney general, 1776–82; Continental Congress delegate, 1779–82; Virginia governor, 1786–88; Constitutional Convention delegate, 1787; U.S. attorney general, 1789–94; U.S. secretary of state, 1794–95

George Washington (1732–1799)
Commander of Continental army, 1775; Continental Congress delegate, 1774–75; presided at Constitutional Convention, 1787; U.S. Constitution signer; U.S. president, 1789–97

For Further INFORMATION

Web Sites

Visit our homepage for lots of links about the Virginia colony:
http://www.childsworld.com/links.html

Note to Parents, Teachers, and Librarians:
We routinely verify our Web links to make sure they're safe,
active sites—so encourage your readers to check them out!

Books

Hossell, Karen Price. *Virginia.* Lucent Books: San Diego, 2001.

Murray, Stuart. *Eyewitness: American Revolution.* New York: DK Publishing, 2002.

Sakurai, Gail. *The Jamestown Colony.* New York: Children's Press, 1997.

Places to Visit or Contact

Association for the Preservation of Virginia Antiquities (APVA)
For information on the APVA's 34 historic properties throughout Virginia, including the Jamestown settlement
204 West Franklin Street
Richmond, VA 23220
804/648-1889

Colonial Williamsburg
To experience Virginia life in the 1700s at the largest outdoor history museum in the country
P.O. Box 1776
Williamsburg, VA 23182-1776
757/229-1000

Index

About the Author

SARAH DECAPUA ENJOYS STUDYING AMERICAN HISTORY— especially the colonial days before the United States gained independence. While researching this book, she enjoyed visiting historic sites in Virginia. Ms. DeCapua works as an editor and author of children's nonfiction books. Born and raised in Connecticut, she now calls Colorado home.